When it's hard to
move

Judith Condon

W
FRANKLIN WATTS
LONDON • SYDNEY

First published in 1998 by
Franklin Watts,
96 Leonard Street,
London EC2A 4XD

Franklin Watts Australia,
56 O'Riordan Street,
Alexandria, Sydney,
NSW 2015

This book was created and
produced for Franklin Watts
by Ruth Nason

Project management: Ruth Nason
Design: Carole Binding
Illustration: Jane Cradock-Watson
Photography: Claire-Maria Cole, Peter Silver
Consultants:Disability Services; Beverley
Matthias/REACH Resource Centre; Dr
Philip Sawney; William Sawney

Printed and bound in Belgium

ISBN 0 7496 4550 4 (pbk)

Dewey Decimal Classification 616.7

Acknowledgements
The author would like
to thank all the people
interviewed for this book:
Ann Begg MP, Ian Bentley,
Rachel Carter, Becky Mason,
Jag Plah, Kirsty Read, Jazmin
Scarlett and family, and Mike
Taylor. Also for their help:
Karen Cox; Kevin Collins, headteacher, and
the children of Great Barr Primary School;
Robina Lloyd; Tom Stone; the London
Transport Unit for Disabled Passengers.

The photographs on page 12 were taken by
Claire-Maria Cole. The photographs on pages
6t, 13, 14l, 15 and 19c were taken by Peter
Silver. Thanks are also expressed to the
following for their permission to reproduce
photographs: Agence France Presse, page 26r;
John Birdsall Photography, pages 17l, 23c;
Richard Bryant/ARCAID, page 6b; Enfield
Mobility Centre, page 25t; Eureka!, page 7t;
Format Photographers, cover br and pages
17r (Brenda Prince), 27b (Jenny Matthews);
David Gold, page 25b; Sally and Richard
Greenhill, pages 7c, 19t, 19c, 22b; London
Transport, page 24; News Team International
Ltd, pages 7b, 18, 19t; Photofusion, pages
16b (David Montford), 19b (David Tothill),
22t (Peter Olive); Jag Plah, page 26l;
Popperfoto, pages 23b, 27t; Science Photo
Library, pages 10 (Andy Levin), 11t (Peter
Menzel), 11b (Dr Gopal Murti), 23t (Hank
Morgan); Mike Taylor, page 14tr and br;
Truly Scrumptious, cover top.

Contents

Introduction

In this book you will meet some people whose movement is limited, or impaired, in some way.

They will tell you about their experiences, and especially about how things can be organized and designed to give them the same opportunities as other people.

▲ Rachel's wheelchair folds so that she can lift it into her car and put it on the back seat.

Designing for all

Do you remember being three, when door handles and sinks were too high to reach and stairs seemed like a mountain to climb? This may help you to think about how frustrating things can seem to a person with a physical impairment. What ways can you think of to make buildings, vehicles and tools easy to use for everyone?

◀ The ramp, the wide spaces and the space under the tables make this canteen easy for someone in a wheelchair to use.

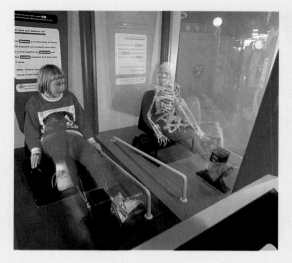

▲ This museum display shows how your bones move as you pedal.

What happens when you move

When you move, the following things happen, all in a fraction of a second:

◆ Your brain forms a plan to move.
◆ Messages from the brain travel, through nerves, to the muscles that will make the movement.
◆ The muscles (which are attached to your bones) work together, some getting shorter and others getting longer, to make the bones move.

Other people's attitudes

Places can be designed to give everyone an equal chance to use them. But people's actions and attitudes are important too. Disabled people want to feel included and equal.

Access

Places made so that disabled people can use them display the 'access' (entry) symbol. The symbol is a wheelchair, but it stands for people with all kinds of disabilities, not just wheelchair users.

◀ Look at all the movement in these children's bodies and faces.

Think about moving

Think about all the parts of your body that move, from your toes to your eyebrows.

Think of the movements this clown made to get dressed in his costume: stretching, pulling, bending, wriggling ... Now try making a list of words for all the types of movement you make as you go through a day.

Some people can move in ways which others cannot. How about you? Can you move your little toe without moving the others, or wink with one eye, or do the splits?

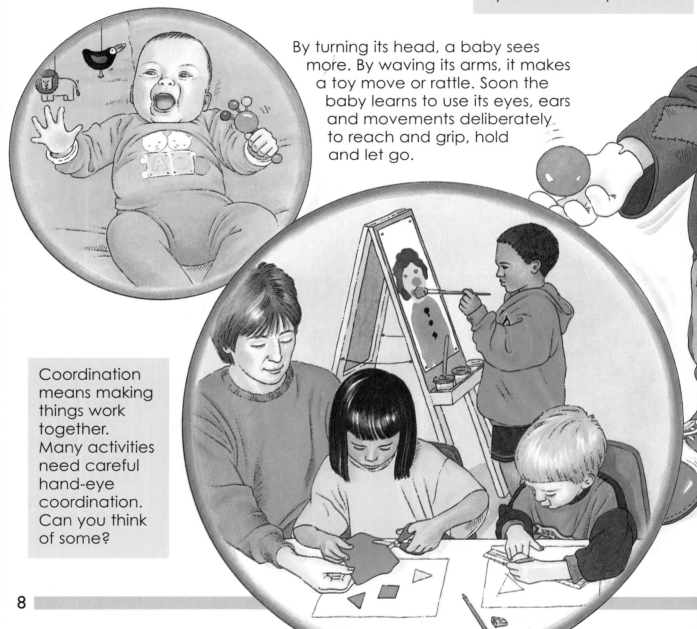

By turning its head, a baby sees more. By waving its arms, it makes a toy move or rattle. Soon the baby learns to use its eyes, ears and movements deliberately to reach and grip, hold and let go.

Coordination means making things work together. Many activities need careful hand-eye coordination. Can you think of some?

Marathon runners train to keep moving over a long distance. Jogging is easier for them than sprinting. Can you think why?

Your ankles, knees and hips bear the weight of your body as you walk or run.

People with impairments take part in marathons and other sports. They may move differently from other people, but they can achieve the same things.

All the time you are awake you are keeping your balance – usually without thinking. To achieve this, your brain uses information from several body senses and sends messages to your muscles.

Causes of impairments

Impairments that affect movement can be caused by damage to the brain, nerves, muscles or bones.

Injury to the brain

Our senses and movements are controlled by different parts of our brain. Injury to the brain may therefore affect sight, hearing, speech, and movement of the arms, legs and face – depending on the part of the brain that is damaged.

Fragile bones

As people grow older, their bones tend to be less strong. This ageing of the bones is called osteoporosis. For some people, it makes the bones break easily.

Injury to the brain called cerebral palsy can happen while a baby is inside its mother, or as a baby is born, or as a result of an illness while a child is very young.

Having cerebral palsy makes some people's movements appear jerky. But, like all impairments, it affects each person in a different way.

◀ Exercises can help a child born with cerebral palsy to learn movement.

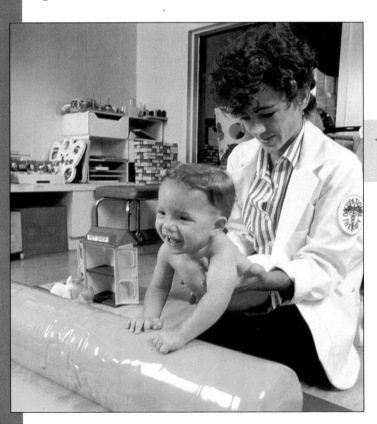

Damage to the nerves

In a disease called multiple sclerosis (MS), damage occurs to the covering around tiny fibres that are part of a person's nerves. It is hard for the nerves to carry messages from the brain to the muscles, and the person has trouble with moving.

The spinal cord

Most messages from the brain to the arms, body and legs travel via the spinal cord, which is protected inside our backbones. An injury to the back may damage the spinal cord and leave the person unable to move in some ways.

▲ Computers controlled by the voice are useful for many disabled people.

▲ A long-handled gripping tool is useful for many everyday tasks.

Painful joints

Joints are where our bones connect. So that our joints move easily, the ends of our bones are covered with a smooth material called cartilage. This slowly wears away, causing some people to feel stiff as they get older – particularly in their hips, knees and spine. This is one type of arthritis.

There are other types of arthritis that can affect children as well as adults.

◄ The top two of these red blood cells are sickle-shaped.

Sickle cell anaemia

Red blood cells are usually round. But in sickle cell anaemia, some of the cells become sickle-shaped. This makes the cells more fragile.

At times, such as in cold weather, the sickle cells clump together and block the blood vessels. This affects the joints, which become very painful.

Losing muscle strength

Some diseases and infections harm and weaken muscles permanently, and so movement is difficult and tiring.

Meet some people
who have trouble with moving

Jazmin Scarlett

Jazmin, aged six and a half, has a rare kind of arthritis.

Most of the time she can run and climb quite happily. But sometimes the arthritis makes it painful for her to move her arms and legs. Her hands swell, so she wears splints to support them.

Jazmin takes pills to stop her joints hurting. Every day she does exercises to help the joints in her feet, legs, shoulders, arms and neck stay supple. She also goes swimming each week. Exercising in the water is good for her – and fun!

▲ As well as playing in the park, Jazmin loves drawing and colouring, and having friends to stay overnight.

Jazmin's arthritis has made her grow more slowly than most children. This is why she is not much taller than her sister Kenya (on the right in the photograph), who is three.

Ian Bentley

Ian has cerebral palsy. He has good eyesight and hearing. But he cannot speak, and he has difficulty walking.

Ian was married and has a daughter. His wife died and now he lives alone. He goes to college, to learn computer skills and creative writing.

Ways of speaking

Ian has an electronic communication aid. By pressing the keys, he makes a recorded voice speak simple messages. He can use this with his telephone.

Computers make it possible to study at home. Instead of travelling to the library, Ian can call up information from the Internet. He can communicate with his teachers using e-mail. But it is still good to get out and meet people.

Ian also points to letters on a board, to spell out what he wants to say.

Meet Mike Taylor ...

Mike was always keen on sport, especially rugby and skiing. One day, out jogging with a friend, he began to limp. It was the start of multiple sclerosis.

Long-distance swimming

Mike formed a six-person team for a sponsored swim from England to France. Each person swam for two hours. The money raised was for research into multiple sclerosis.

Mike (preparing to swim, above, and in the water, below) was the only disabled swimmer. He wore buoyancy shorts to help keep his legs in position.

Mike's team has also swum the length of Loch Lomond in Scotland.

'The toughest thing was telling my parents,' Mike says. 'Some of my friends don't know what to say. They don't get in touch any more. But as some doors close, others start to open!'

Mike is a designer of printed material, such as books and posters. He stopped travelling to his office to work, and now works at home.

Although Mike cannot walk unaided, he likes swimming. He has found that his muscles work better in cold water.

... and Becky Mason

Becky drives a vehicle that has been adapted for her needs.

Her wheelchair fits on to the side lift, which she lowers and raises by remote control.

Becky's spine was badly injured in a car accident when she was 17, and she was in hospital for a year. Her injury has left her unable to walk.

▲ Becky's vehicle has automatic gears, and the brakes are worked by hand.

After the accident, Becky completed her studies at school. She went to university, where she studied Maths, then Management.

Now Becky is a manager for a big telephone company. Her work includes answering questions from workers all around the country.

Becky is buying her own house. In her spare time she loves to go out with friends. She enjoys sports, and goes bob-skiing and water-skiing, using skis that allow her to sit rather than stand.

◀ Becky works in an open-plan office like the one on pages 20-21.

At home

Home is where everyone likes to feel comfortable and cared about.

Homes that suit

Homes can be made to suit the needs of people who have physical impairments. For example, surfaces in the kitchen may need a space underneath where a wheelchair user's legs can fit. Shelves, handles, switches and many other items need to be placed where they are easy to reach.

▶ This 'multi-purpose turner' is for people who find it hard to grip and turn something fiddly, like a key.

◀ Most of the comfort of home comes from the love of family and friends.

Support for disabled people

Disabled people may need personal help with some parts of day-to-day life. Sometimes this can come from family or friends.

Also, a law has been passed granting money to disabled people so that they can pay personal assistants to give them the support they want. This allows people to stay independent and in control of their lives.

A stair lift makes it easy to get up and down stairs.

Moving about

For some people, including wheelchair users and those who walk with the aid of sticks or a walking frame, it is hard to get up and down steps. It is easier to use a ramp (a shallow slope). At home, some disabled people may have a ramp to their front or back door.

Indoors, for example by the stairs or in the bathroom, people may need hand rails to hold on to when standing or walking.

Some people need a hoist or a seat that goes up and down, for getting into bed or into the bath.

Wheelchairs can be adapted in many ways to suit their users.

Wheelchairs

Some wheelchairs are driven by hand – turning the large back wheels. Heavier chairs have a battery-driven motor. Both kinds can also be pushed. But never push a wheelchair without asking the person if he or she would like you to.

Some wheelchair users have a 'wheel-cleaner' outside their homes. Do you know why?

Useful tools for everyone

A TV remote control and an electric tin-opener are useful tools for everyone – and perhaps particularly for people who have trouble with moving. Can you think of other tools that are useful for everyone?

At school and college

Keeping fit

All children need exercise to keep fit. Sometimes children with a physical impairment join in with PE lessons. Some schools have special physiotherapy equipment for them to use.

◀ A desk is designed to fit with a wheelchair.

The pictures on this page were taken at a school where 23 of the 450 children have some kind of physical impairment.

Think about what a school needs to do, to be sure that children with impairments have equal chances with others.

In the playground

Here's Kamaldeep Singh arriving at school. Sometimes he uses sticks and sometimes he uses a wheelchair. Kamaldeep says: 'One problem is in the playground, where people are running around. There are rules about wheelchairs, such as no wheelies, no skidding and no running. But sometimes friends run with us, and then we get into trouble!'

Dolls

This school's store of toys includes some dolls with wheelchairs, walking frames or crutches. All these items are modelled on the equipment that some people use in real life.

Kirsty's story

Kirsty Read (left) is at university, studying English. She has been disabled since birth.

She remembers: 'When I started school, I was the first child in a wheelchair that the school had ever had. It opened the way for others. Everyone was learning, including the teachers.

'At my next school, my mum got two lifts built, so that I could get to the upper floors.'

At university, Kirsty has her own room, and two personal assistants who take turns to give her support. She says:

'Everyone here is really good. They don't treat me differently from anyone else. I enjoy university a lot – and you can do better at something you enjoy.'

▶ Swimming gives confidence and a sense of freedom. This pool is at a school for children with physical impairments.

At work

The main picture here shows a work place planned to be safe and comfortable for all. It is light and airy, with plenty of space. There is a canteen and recreation room. The whole area is smoke-free.

Can you see some things that are specially helpful to people whose movement is limited?

The picture below shows a poorly organized work place where accidents could occur. There are trailing wires. Files could topple from the shelves. The man is likely to develop a stiff neck from holding the telephone between his shoulder and chin.

In Britain a law says that employers must not treat disabled people less fairly than others. They must make reasonable changes to the workplace in order to give access to disabled workers.

What equipment has been provided for lifting and carrying heavy items?

A head-set and mouthpiece allow this telephone user to sit comfortably, with his hands free.

A trained therapist gives shoulder massage to relieve stiffness.

Doors are automatic, and there are lifts to the upper floors.

Staff have been trained to bend at the knee to pick up something heavy, so that they do not strain their backs.

The wide-doored toilet is for disabled people. Inside there is space for a wheelchair and hand rails are at a convenient height.

Keyboard operators take breaks, to prevent straining their hands and wrists.

The work place consists of small units, linked by wide covered walkways. Each unit has its own parking area.

Tables have rounded corners, and the height of chairs can be adjusted.

There are ramps instead of steps.

Keeping fit

Regular exercise helps keep muscles toned and joints flexible. It strengthens the heart, and is good for the circulation of blood round the body.

The pictures here show some of the ways in which people with restricted movement enjoy keeping fit.

Horse-riding

Kirsten (right) has spina bifida, which makes walking difficult for her. She enjoys the fun and fresh air of riding.

▲ Volunteer guides for an organization called Riding for the Disabled take Kirsten on her favourite horse, Fudge.

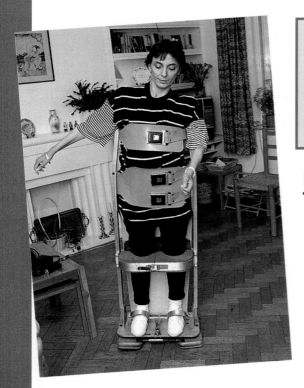

Swimming clubs

Many towns have swimming clubs for disabled people. Does your local pool have a hoist for helping disabled swimmers get into the water?

Keeping fit at home

Sitting for a long time in the same chair can cause sores to develop where the skin is pressed. It can also restrict blood circulation. Celeste (left) has a standing frame which allows her to exercise out of her wheelchair. She moves along by rocking her weight from side to side.

A sports club

Snowy weather does not stop these members of a sports club for disabled people. But a person in a wheelchair must wrap up especially warm. A person sitting always feel colder than people who are walking or running.

Ball games

Many ball games, including cricket, basket-ball and volley-ball, are played fast and furiously by wheelchair users.

▼ Racing wheelchairs are light and have no brakes.

Champion athletes

At the Paralympics (the Olympic Games for disabled people) in Atlanta in 1996, David Holding of Britain (right in the photograph) set a world record in the men's 100 metres. The runner-up was Hakan Eriksson of Sweden.

Out and about

Being able to travel allows people to meet, to have fun, and to take up opportunities at college and at work.

Many public transport companies have improved their vehicles and services to ensure that disabled people can travel where and when they wish. But there are still lots of improvements to make.

Having a say

Disabled people themselves should have a say when new buildings are designed and new services are offered. They know better than anyone else what is needed and how it should be provided.

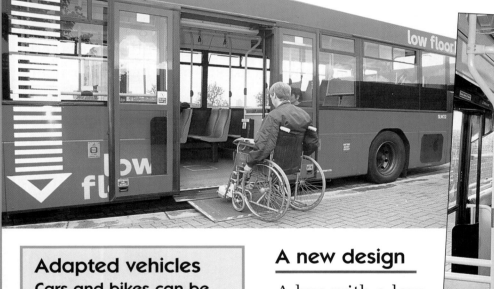

Adapted vehicles

Cars and bikes can be adapted in many ways to suit individual users. For example, some bikes can be pedalled with the hands instead of the feet.

A new design

A bus with a low floor is easier for everyone to climb into and out of. This one also has a ramp. The driver can make it slide out, for any passengers who need it.

Inside, a space for a wheelchair user has a back rest to help make the ride less bumpy.

Parking

Car parks have spaces for disabled drivers, near to the entrance. In some towns, disabled drivers and passengers are given a badge to display in their cars when they park. This permits them to park in 'No Parking' areas, near to where they want to go.

Going shopping

Some towns have a shop-mobility centre where people who find it hard to walk can borrow from a range of scooters and buggies, to go shopping. Other useful things in towns are flattened kerbs, and automatic doors.

A wheelchair 'for best'

Ann Begg was elected Member of Parliament for Aberdeen, Scotland, in 1997. Before that she was a teacher. She uses a wheelchair to go about her work. It can be hoisted into a storage space on top of her car.

'The wheelchair gets pretty battered,' Ann says, 'so I've bought a new posh one with gold-plated bits for special occasions. After all, you wouldn't wear scruffy old shoes with your best clothes, would you?'

As an MP, Ann travels between Scotland and London each week. She has also been to Egypt, and went by helicopter to visit an oil rig in the North Sea.

Famous people

Isabella Bird (1831-1904)

Isabella developed disease of the spine as a girl and suffered pain for the rest of her life. Yet, in an age when most women hardly went beyond their family circle, Isabella became an explorer. She travelled by horse, yak, camel or elephant in Mexico, China, Japan, Malaysia and Persia (now Iran), and wrote books about her experiences.

Land mines

Land mines are bombs hidden in the earth during wars. After the war, danger from the mines remains, especially if no one recorded where the mines were laid. As people walk over them, or dig the fields, the mines explode. They cause terrible injury, in many cases leaving people disabled.

▶ Princess Diana talks to Mirzeta Gabelic, who was injured by a land mine in Bosnia. The Princess tried to convince people to stop making these weapons.

Jag Plah (born 1957)

Jag is an actor, comedian and writer. He says his first try at acting, at age 8, was in a school Nativity play. He was so nervous that he was sick and could not go on! In 1980, Jag, who has cerebral palsy, helped start the Graeae Theatre Company, made up of disabled actors, and they went on tour to the USA. Jag says that the best way to get good parts is to write plays himself. He also plans to write a story about going to the moon.

Christopher Reeve (born 1952)

Christopher became famous from acting in the *Superman* films. Then a horse-riding accident left him unable to move from the neck down. He has begun a new career as a film director.

► Christopher Reeve with his wife and daughter.

Pierre Auguste Renoir (1841-1919)

Renoir was an artist who painted sunny scenes of Paris and the French countryside. In his later years he had arthritis, and worked with his paintbrush strapped to his hand.

◄ Some people without the use of their hands learn to hold things skilfully with their mouth and feet. This young woman is at a painting class.

Mouth and Foot Painting Artists
About 400 artists, from 56 countries, belong to the Association of Mouth and Foot Painting Artists. By selling the artists' work, the organization makes enough money to pay its members a monthly income for the whole of their lives. It also pays for new mouth and foot painters to be trained.

Franklin Delano Roosevelt (1882-1945)

Roosevelt was President of the USA from 1933 to 1945. He had caught polio in 1922, and this illness left him unable to move his legs. In photographs, Roosevelt was often shown only from the waist upwards. In 1998, disabled Americans campaigned successfully for a new statue of Roosevelt to be made, showing him in his wheelchair.

Glossary

Some conditions causing physical impairment are described on pages 10-11. Others mentioned in the text are explained briefly in this Glossary.

arthritis

There are several types of arthritis. Osteo-arthritis is caused by wear and tear. The cartilage covering the ends of bones wears away. Another kind of arthritis is part of an illness that affects the whole body, causing rashes and fever as well as stiffness in the joints. Many people think arthritis affects only older people. In fact, one in 1,000 children have arthritis. Some are much better by the time they are adults.

muscular dystrophy (MD)

an inherited condition, more likely to affect boys than girls, which affects the ability to use the muscles for movement. Gradually, the muscles get weaker and waste away.

Dyspraxia

For unknown reasons, some children have problems with movement that make them appear clumsy or unco-ordinated, though they are just as intelligent as other children. This is called dyspraxia. It can also affect the child's speaking.

osteoporosis

This is sometimes called 'brittle bones'. 'Osteo' means to do with bones. 'Porosis' refers to their porous texture. Many older people, especially women, develop this condition, which makes them lose several inches in height. Sometimes their bones are so fragile that they break after just a knock. Some younger people have an inherited form of this condition.

physiotherapy

exercises and sometimes massage, used not only to treat long-term impairment, but also after an accident, where bones or muscles have been hurt, or after a person has been confined to bed for a long time. Many sports people have regular physiotherapy because of the strains and injuries they receive.

polio (poliomyelitis)

an infectious disease of the nerves in the spine. There was an epidemic of polio in Britain and the USA in the 1940s and 1950s. Children now are vaccinated against it.

spina bifida

a condition in which a baby's backbone does not form completely before the baby is born. This leaves part of the spinal cord unprotected, affecting the child's ability to move.

Useful information

Eureka! the museum for children,

Discovery Road,
Halifax HX1 2NE
tel 01422 330069
This museum with a fun, participatory approach has a 'What if I Couldn't?' section focusing on what it is like to be disabled.

Dolls and realistic aids

(as on page 19) are available from:
NES Arnold Ltd,
Ludlow Hill Road,
West Bridgford,
Nottingham NG2 6HD
tel 0115 971 7700
(Export: 44-115 945 2204)

Children's fiction

The following recommended books include characters who are disabled:
Jean and Gareth Adamson, *Topsy and Tim and Their New School Friend* (Puffin Books)
Michael Foreman, *Seal Surfer* (Andersen Press)
Emily Hearn, *Race You Franny*, *Good Morning Franny* and *Franny and the Music Girl* (Magi Publications)
David Hill, *See Ya Simon* (Puffin Books)
Julie Johnston, *Hero of Lesser Causes* (Orchard Books)
Jean Little, *Mine for Keeps* (Viking)

Educational videos

(Suitable for secondary-age children and for disability awareness training)
Altogether Better (about inclusive education), by M. Mason and R. Reiser, is available from:
Comic Relief Education,
Unit 2, Drywall Estate,
Castle Road,
Sittingbourne,
Kent ME10 3RL

We're Here Too (presented by young disabled people) is available from:
Individeo Ltd,
80 Mildmay Grove,
London N1 4PJ

Organizations

Organizations offering information with particular reference to children include:
Children's Chronic Arthritis Association,
47 Battenhall Avenue,
Worcester WR5 2HN
tel 01905 763556

Dyspraxia Foundation,
8 West Alley, Hitchin,
Herts SG5 1EG
tel 01462 454986

The Muscular Dystrophy Group,
7-11 Prescott Place,
London SW4 6BS
tel 0171 720 8055

The Sickle Cell Society,
54 Station Road,
London NW10 4UA
tel 0181 961 7795

IN AUSTRALIA
Muscular Dystrophy Association, Royal South Sydney Community Health Complex, Joynton Avenue, Zetland N.S.W. 2017

Index

How to look after your bones

◆ **Drink lots of milk and eat foods rich in calcium, in order to develop strong bones.**

◆ **Take regular brisk walks and play games involving running and jumping, to keep bones strong.**

◆ **Never smoke. People who smoke are much more likely to get brittle bones.**

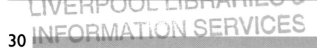